Musical Instruments

Xylophone

By Nick Rebman

level 1
little blue readers

www.littlebluehousebooks.com

Little Blue House is distributed by North Star Editions:
sales@northstareditions.com | 888-417-0195

Produced for Little Blue House by Red Line Editorial.

Photographs ©: Shutterstock Images, cover, 7, 10–11, 15, 17, 19, 23, 24 (top left), 24 (top right); iStockphoto, 4, 9, 13, 21, 24 (bottom left), 24 (bottom right)

Library of Congress Control Number: 2022911116

ISBN
978-1-64619-705-7 (hardcover)
978-1-64619-737-8 (paperback)
978-1-64619-798-9 (ebook pdf)
978-1-64619-769-9 (hosted ebook)

Printed in the United States of America
Mankato, MN
012023

About the Author

Nick Rebman is a writer and editor who lives in Minnesota. He enjoys reading, walking his dog, and playing rock songs on his drum set.

Table of Contents

Playing the Xylophone

I play the xylophone.

It makes a nice sound.

The xylophone has
many bars.
The bars are made
of wood.

bar

I hold two mallets in my hands.
I use the mallets to hit the bars.

mallet

The large bars make low notes.

The small bars make high notes.

My teacher shows me how to play.
She tells me which bars to hit.

teacher

I learn how to read
sheet music.
I start playing slowly.

sheet music

I practice every day.

I get better and better.

Soon I can play faster.

I learn many
different songs.
I play them again
and again.

I like to play with my friends. Sometimes we play outside.

Glossary

bars

sheet music

mallets

teacher

Index